DISCOVER
Volcanoes & Earthquakes

Contributing Writer
Martin F. J. Flower, Ph.D.

Consultant
Bruce A. Bolt, Ph.D.

Publications International, Ltd.

Copyright © 1992 Publications International, Ltd. All rights reserved. This publication may not be reproduced or quoted in whole or in part by mimeograph or any other printed or electronic means, or for presentation on radio, television, videotape, or film without written permission from:

Louis Weber, C.E.O.
Publications International, Ltd.
7373 N. Cicero Avenue
Lincolnwood, Illinois 60646

Permission is never granted for commercial purposes.

Manufactured in USA

8 7 6 5 4 3 2 1

ISBN 1-56173-423-3

Photo Credits

Front cover: **Comstock** (center & bottom right); **Glenn M. Oliver/Eagle River Media Productions** (top right & right center).

Back cover: **Tom & Michele Grimm/International Stock Photography** (bottom); **D. Marklin/FPG International** (top).

Animals Animals: 28 (top), 36 (top); **Comstock:** Front endsheet (top right), 6 (bottom), 9 (top), 11 (top), 18 (bottom), 26 (top & center), 31 (center); **Earthquake Engineering Research Institute:** 43 (top & center), back endsheet (center); **Michael Everett/D. Donne Bryant Stock Photography Agency:** 24 (top); **FPG International:** Table of contents (top), 20 (center), back endsheet (top left); Paul Ambrose: 35 (top); Nancy Cataldi: 17 (top), 36 (center); Willard Clay: 18 (top), back endsheet (bottom right); Gerald L. French: 30 (bottom); Harold W. Gosline & M. Romana: 24 (bottom); Larry Grant: 32 (bottom), 33 (top), back endsheet (bottom left; Peter Gridley: 13 (top); Dennis Hallinan: Front endsheet (center); Max & Bea Hunn: 16 (top); Franz Lazi: 21 (bottom); Patricia Pomtili: 35 (center); Gary Randall: 19 (bottom); Michael Tamborrino: 42 (top); The Telegraph Colour Library: 5, 30 (center), 34 (top); Ron Thomas: 39 (top right); Jack Zehrt: 1; **International Stock Photography:** Tom Carroll Photography: 12 (center), 29 (top), 32 (top & center); Dennis Fisher: 11 (bottom); Tom & Michele Grimm: 19 (top); Michael J. Howell: 40 (top); Miwako Ikeda: 13 (bottom), 41 (bottom); Horst Oesterwinter: Front endsheet (top left); Dario Perla: 12 (top), 30 (top); Jonathan E. Pite: 41 (bottom); Robert C. Russell: 20 (bottom); Elliott Smith: 27 (bottom left), 33 (bottom), 36 (bottom), 40 (center); **Gary Milburn/Tom Stack & Associates:** 33 (center); **National Geophysical Data Center:** Table of contents (bottom right), 6 (top), 7 (bottom), 12 (bottom), 17 (bottom), 21 (top left & top right), 22, 23 (top), 29 (center & bottom), 34 (bottom left & bottom right), 35 (bottom), 38 (top), 39 (bottom), 41 (center), 42 (center), 43 (bottom); **Glenn M. Oliver/Eagle River Media Productions:** Table of contents (bottom left), 23 (left center), 25 (center), 42 (bottom); **Rainbow:** Christiana Dittmann: 8 (top); Dan McCoy: Back endsheet (top right); Hank Morgan: 9 (bottom); **Harald Sund/The Image Bank:** 11 (bottom left); **U.S. Geological Survey:** Front end sheet (bottom left & bottom right), table of contents (left center & right center), 4, 7 (top left & top right), 16 (bottom), 17 (center), 20 (top), 22, 23 (right center & bottom), 24 (center), 25 (bottom), 26 (bottom), 37, 38 (center & bottom), 39 (top left & center), 40 (bottom); **Robin White/FotoLex:** 25 (top), 28 (bottom right), 31 (bottom).

Illustrations: Lorie Robare; Steve Fuller

Martin F. J. Flower holds a Ph.D. in volcanology/geochemistry from the University of Manchester, U.K. He is a former editorial board member of *Geology* magazine and was a research associate for the Smithsonian Institution, Museum of Natural History. He is managing editor of *Earth Science Reviews* and is a professor of geological sciences at the University of Illinois, Chicago.

Bruce A. Bolt, Ph.D. has been professor of seismology at the University of California since 1963. He has been president of both the International Association of Seismology and the Seismological Society of America. He is recognized as a major educator in the U.S. and abroad in earthquake science, and has written several popular textbooks.

Editorial assistance: Jennifer Vogelgesang

CONTENTS

OUR RESTLESS EARTH • 4
The Earth's Layers • Plate Tectonics • Plate Boundaries •
Hot Spots

VOLCANOES • 14
The Pacific Ring of Fire • Famous Volcanic Eruptions •
Structure of a Volcano • Types of Volcanic Eruptions •
What Comes Out of Volcanoes •
Side Effects of Eruptions

EARTHQUAKES • 26
Faults • Structure of an Earthquake • Measuring
Earthquakes • Tsunamis • Famous Earthquakes

LIVING WITH DANGER • 36
Studying the Earth • Predicting Eruptions • Predicting
Earthquakes • Protecting Against Disaster •
After a Disaster

GLOSSARY • 44

Our Restless Earth

is in many ways a living body. It changes all the time. And it has many forms of energy, some of which we need to live.

Now and then people can see and feel the earth's energy. They watch mountain-shaped volcanoes explode, or erupt. They feel earthquakes shake the ground beneath them. Maybe you have seen or felt these things—or maybe you have learned about them through newspapers and television.

Volcanoes and earthquakes are signs that our planet is working. They are signs that powerful forces are shaping the earth from the inside out. Volcanoes and earthquakes show us the earth is awake and restless and very much alive.

THE EARTH'S LAYERS

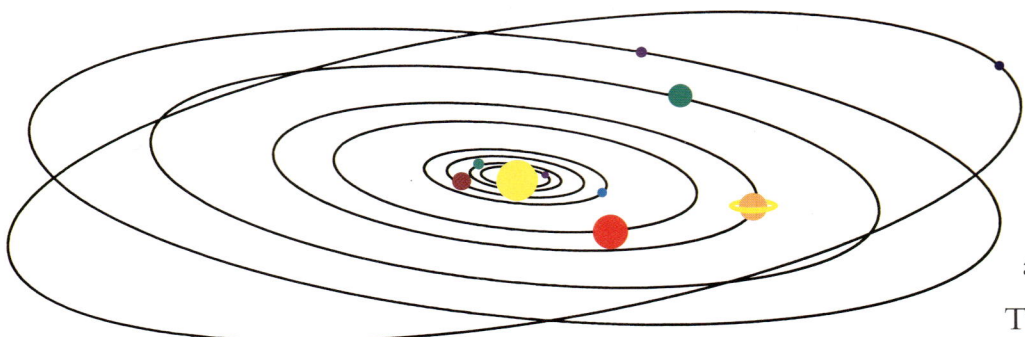

Earth is one of the planets of our solar system. The solar system is made up of the sun, nine planets, and all the moons that move around the planets. Our earth is really an amazing planet.

The earth is very big. If you dug a hole from the earth's surface to its center, that hole would be 4,000 miles deep! That's just about the distance from San Francisco, California, to Washington, D.C.—and back again!

Our planet earth is one of the nine planets in the solar system.

The earth can be a very exciting place to live.

The earth is also very, very old. Scientists think it is over four billion years old! Scientists have discovered other things about our planet. For example, they know the earth has layers, just like a birthday cake.

Each layer is made up of different kinds of rocks that have different weights. Rocks in the earth's middle are heavier than rocks near its surface.

The picture we have of the earth's inside structure is quite simple. Scientists believe our planet began as a cloud of hot gases mixed together. The cloud was part of the Solar Nebula (NEB-yuh-luh), a huge cloud of hot gas and dust. As the nebula cloud whirled around the sun, gases in the cloud began spinning off on their own. The gases cooled over time to become solid "balls," or planets.

The nebula from which our solar system formed might have looked very much like this.

As the earth cooled, it separated into three main layers. The *core* is at the center of the earth. The *crust* is the planet's outer skin. And the *mantle* is between the core and the crust.

The Core

The earth's core is split into two parts—an inner and an outer core. Scientists have learned that the inner core is solid and that the outer core is liquid.

The Mantle

The mantle surrounds the core and takes up the most space inside our planet. It is completely solid. Even so, strong heat and pressure inside the earth cause it to shift around, just like the liquid core. Later, we'll see how the moving mantle causes volcanoes and earthquakes.

The Crust

Rocks in the crust are cool. They are brittle. This means that they will break, like hard candy, when pressure is applied to them. The rocks may break and shatter to form long cracks called *faults*.

Sometimes faults extend all the way through the crust to the mantle. When this happens, the faults may form pathways for gas, heat, and *magma* (MAG-muh) to escape to the surface through volcanoes. Magma is hot, molten rock from the mantle.

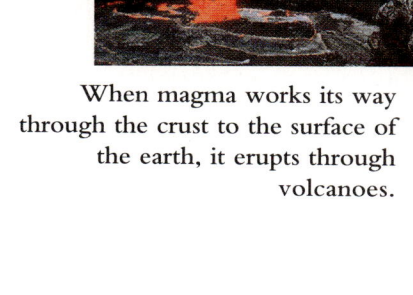

When magma works its way through the crust to the surface of the earth, it erupts through volcanoes.

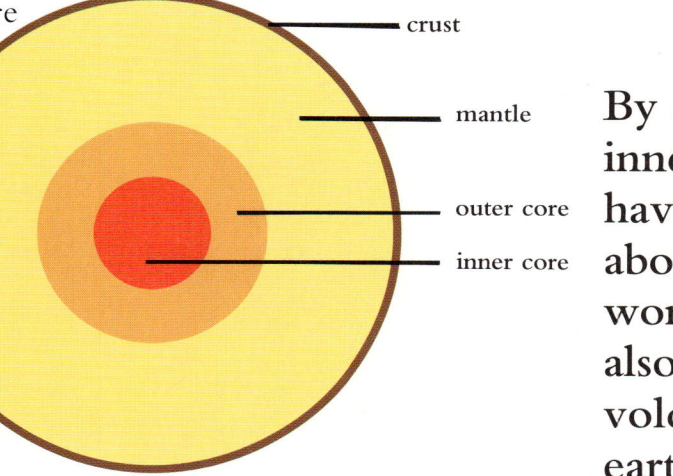

By studying the earth's inner layers, scientists have learned more about how the earth works. They have also learned how volcanoes and earthquakes happen.

Magma is red-hot and liquid when it reaches the surface. Later, it will cool into solid rock.

PLATE TECTONICS

This photo shows the center of Australia. Millions of years ago, this island continent was joined to Antarctica and formed part of one giant continent.

If you look at a globe or map of the earth you will see some familiar patterns. Imagine the earth as a giant puzzle.

Look at Europe and Africa. See how they may fit together with North and South America? You can also see how India, Australia, Antarctica, and east Africa may also fit together.

Scientists tell us these large pieces of land, called continents, once did fit together. Millions of years ago, they formed one giant continent. Pieces of this great continent have moved apart through the ages and are still moving today.

This movement is very, very slow. It takes thousands of years for a continent to move just a few feet. Still, a map made today will look much different from a map made in a million years.

What forces make the continents move? Millions of years ago, the earth's crust cracked into several pieces. As the mantle shifts around, it pushes and pulls the chunks of crust in different directions. The broken pieces of crust actually ride on broken pieces of the mantle's outer edge beneath them.

The chunks of crust, along with the pieces of mantle under them, are called *tectonic plates* (tek-TAHN-ik playts). "Tectonic" comes from a Greek word that means "builder." Tectonic plates build and rebuild the earth's surface as they move over the shifting mantle. The study of moving plates is called *plate tectonics*.

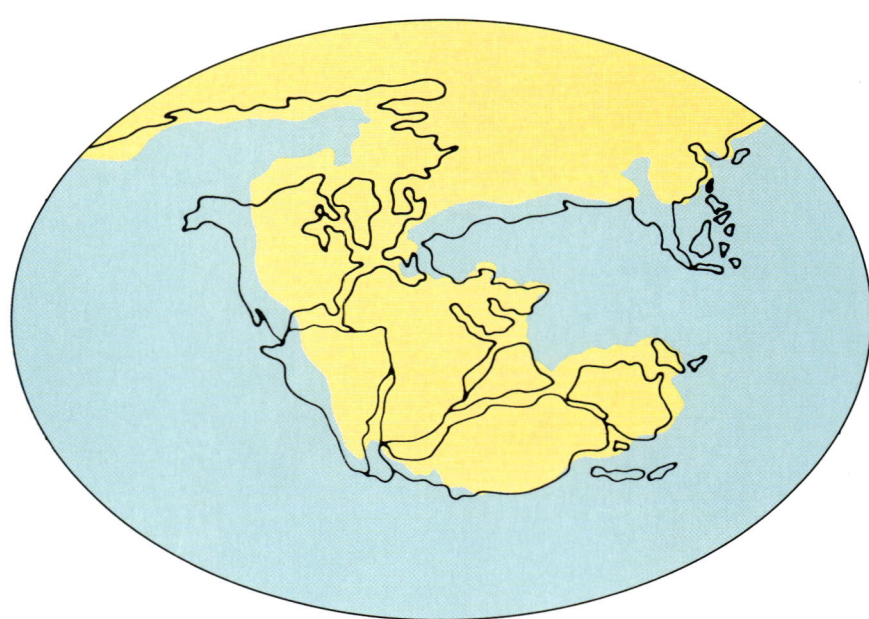

This map shows the earth as it looked millions of years ago when there was just one enormous continent. The outlines show today's continents and how they fitted together.

8

We know about seven major tectonic plates on the earth's surface. These are the North American, South American, Pacific, Australian, African, Eurasian, and Antarctic plates. Some plates include just landmasses. Others also include oceans. In addition to these, there are a few small plates.

The Australian plate contains Australia, India, and the northeastern Indian Ocean. The Eurasian plate contains Europe and most of Asia. It moves slowly to the east. Some eighty million years ago, India "crashed" into Eurasia. The crash squeezed up huge amounts of rock to form the Himalayan mountains. Many mountain ranges were formed by ancient plates crashing together.

Antarctica sits on a plate that is actually growing.

Cracks in the earth's crust, at the edges of plates, are called faults. When faults shift, they cause earthquakes.

The Appalachian mountains were formed when two plates crashed together.

The African plate holds the continent of Africa and parts of the Atlantic and Indian Oceans. It is moving eastward and northward. The Antarctic plate is actually growing larger. The Pacific Ocean is surrounded by plates moving inward. It is probably shrinking.

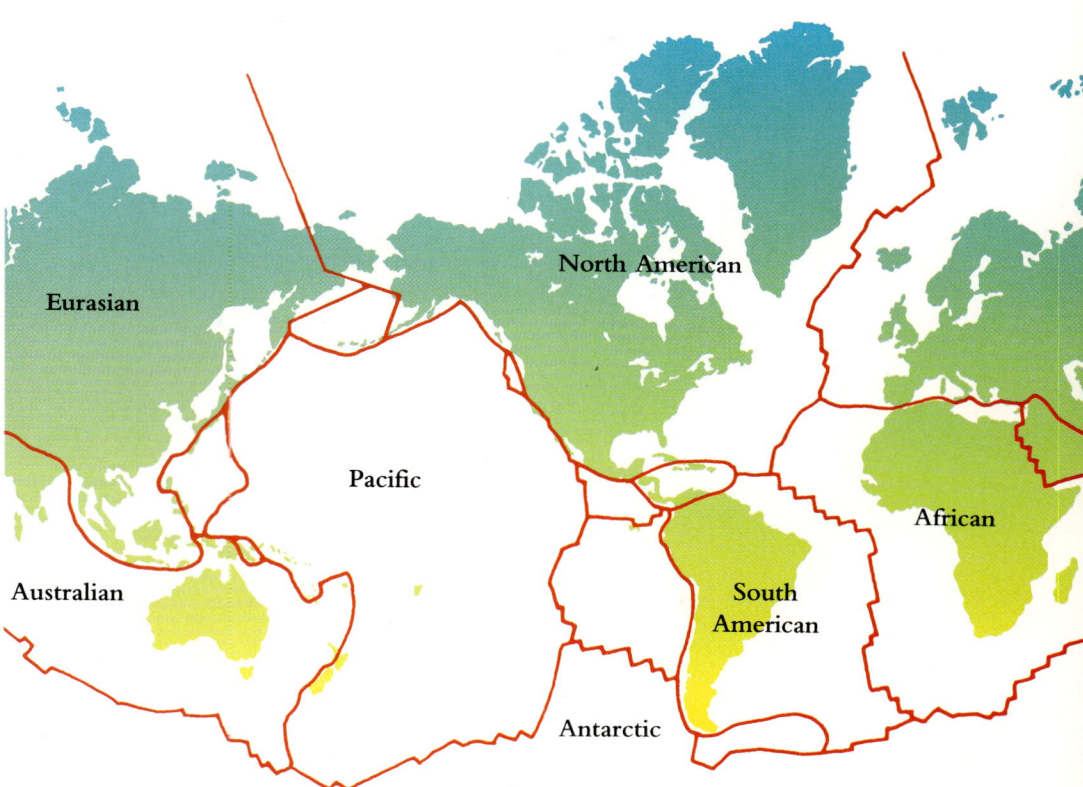

This map shows the boundaries between the major tectonic plates.

PLATE BOUNDARIES

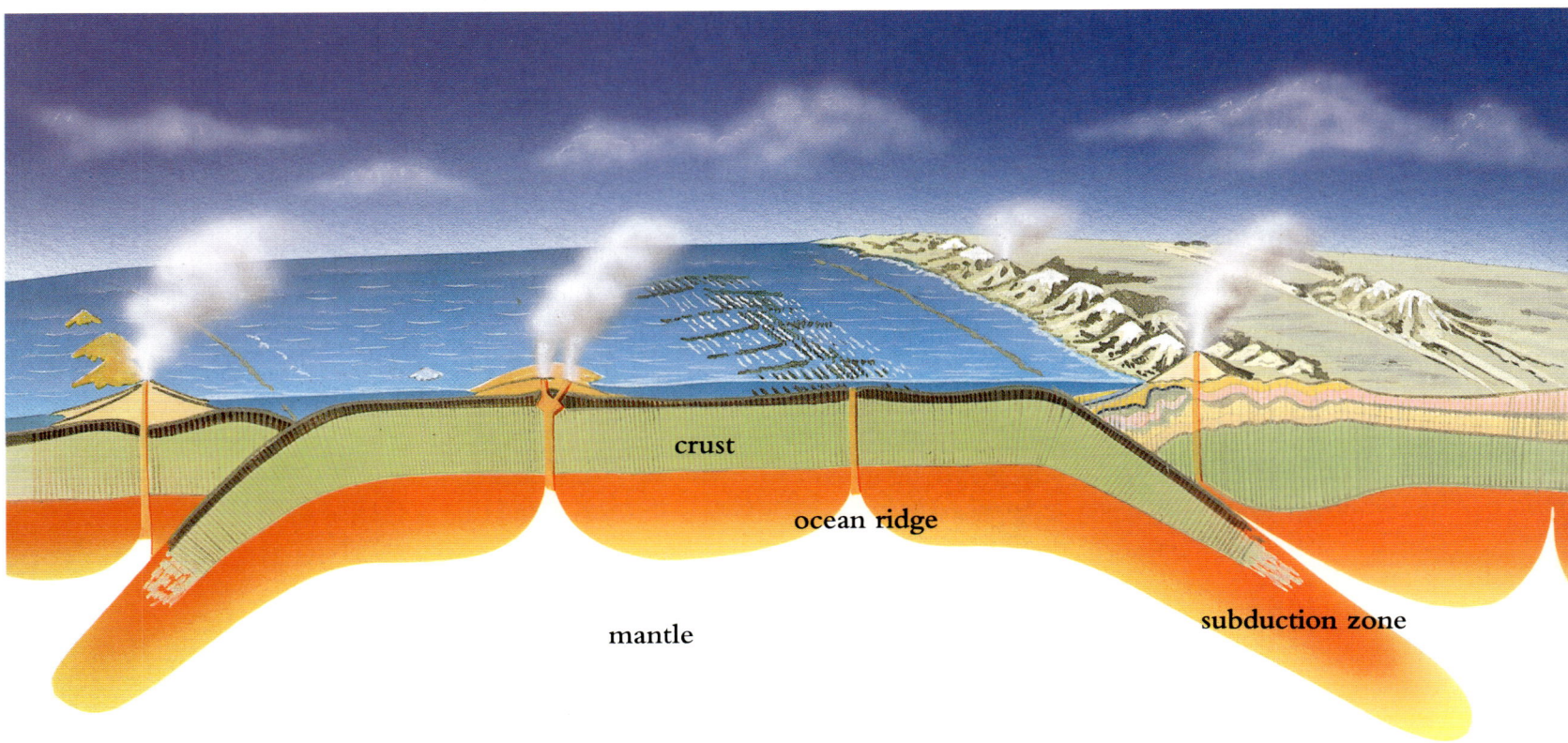

Tectonic plates move away from each other at ocean ridges. At subduction zones, plates collide and one dives under the other. This activity forms mountain ranges and volcanoes. It also causes earthquakes.

Ocean ridges stretch around the earth and are often as high as mountains on land.

The places where tectonic plates touch each other are called *plate boundaries*. There are three types of plate boundaries.

Ocean Ridges

Just as the continents have mountain ranges, so do the oceans. They form along ocean floors, way down deep. Scientists have studied these from ships and submarines.

The underwater mountains rise up at places where plates are moving away from each other. This kind of plate boundary is called an *ocean ridge*. As the plates pull away from each other, magma squeezes up from the mantle to fill the space between the plates. The magma erupts through underwater volcanoes.

The magma forms a solid ridge when it reaches the ocean floor. In this way, ridges of ocean mountains separate some plates. The plates pull away from the ocean ridges that form between them. This is known as *sea-floor spreading*. As the plates continue to move apart, cooled magma sticks to their edges. This is how new crust is formed.

Subduction Zones

A tectonic plate may travel for hundreds of millions of years. It may bump against another plate moving in the opposite direction. This other plate is moving away from an ocean ridge beyond it.

When plates collide, one of them gives way. Its edge sinks beneath the other plate, back down into the mantle. This process is called *subduction* (suhb-DUHK-shuhn).

As subduction occurs, curved valleys several miles deep form in the ocean floor. Lines of volcanoes often erupt behind these valleys, which mark *subduction zones*. Some subduction zones occur in the Atlantic, Pacific, and Indian Oceans.

Subduction zone volcanoes are very explosive. They release steam, a fine-grained, dustlike material called *ash*, and many types of magma. Well-known volcanoes of this type occur in Japan (Mount Fujiyama),

southeast Asia (Krakatoa), western North America (Mount St. Helens), and the Mediterranean (Mount Vesuvius, Mount Etna, Santorini).

The volcano Arenal, in Costa Rica, is a subduction-zone volcano. It is near the place where the small Cocos plate collides with the North American plate.

Subduction-zone volcanoes are tall, smooth cones.

The Cascade Mountain Range in Oregon and Washington is really a line of ancient volcanoes formed at the subduction zone where the Pacific and North American plates meet.

PLATE BOUNDARIES

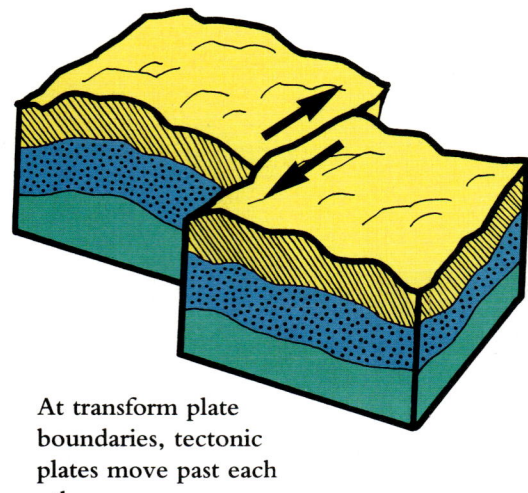

At transform plate boundaries, tectonic plates move past each other.

The San Andreas Fault, and the smaller faults that branch off from it, can be seen at the surface.

Transform Plate Boundaries

When scientists see ocean ridges, they know they are looking at places where two plates are moving apart. When they see subduction zones, they know they're looking at places where two plates push together.

Another type of plate boundary forms where two plates scrape sideways alongside each other at their edges instead of bumping together or pulling apart. This is called a *transform plate boundary*. Faults form along these boundaries.

One of the most famous examples of a transform plate boundary is the San Andreas Fault. It is in California. This fault has formed between the North American and the Pacific plates. East of the fault is the North American plate. The Pacific plate lies west of the fault. These plates are moving along each other in different directions.

Measurements taken during past earthquakes tell us this fault cuts right down to the mantle. The North American plate moves an average of about an inch and a half each year against the Pacific plate.

This does not happen all the time, though. And without movement, pressure may build for many years. Then, the fault's boundaries move many yards in a short time—and an earthquake occurs!

The San Andreas Fault runs through the whole state of California. It has caused earthquakes in Los Angeles, San Francisco, and many places between.

San Francisco is a big city. A strong earthquake could cause much damage here.

The San Andreas Fault is just one place where the North and South American plates move against the Pacific plate. The Mexico City earthquake of 1985 was caused by a movement along the boundaries of these plates.

HOT SPOTS

Some volcanoes are far from plate boundaries. They are not caused by plates moving apart or crashing into each other. These volcanoes often form ocean islands. Examples of volcanic ocean islands include Hawaii, Iceland, and the Galapagos Islands.

What produces these volcanoes? Scientists believe the island-forming volcanoes erupt when extra-hot spots in the mantle rise to the base of a plate. The hot spots cause magma to form and force its way to the surface through volcanoes. This type of activity is called *hot-spot volcanism*.

If you look at a map showing where earthquakes and volcanoes have occurred, you will see that most occur around the Pacific Ocean and throughout the Mediterranean Sea. Lines of earthquakes also run along ocean ridges and some other cracks in the earth's crust. These places mark the main boundaries between plates.

This explains why a country like Japan has great earthquakes and explosive volcanoes. Japan is located where two plates come together. The same goes for Greece, Italy, and South America, all of which have volcanoes and earthquake activity.

Every year, visitors come to Hawaii to enjoy the ocean and the beautiful beaches. Many of them don't realize that they are sunbathing above a huge mantle hot spot.

The Hawaiian Island chain is far from any plate boundaries. It was formed by hot-spot volcanism.

Mount Fujiyama, in Japan, is not a hot-spot volcano. It is caused by a subduction zone nearby. This subduction zone also causes frequent earthquakes.

13

Volcanoes

are one of nature's most dramatic happenings. They hiss and roar with steam. Our word "volcano" comes from the name of an island near Italy (Vulcano). The island's rumbling, erupting mountain was thought to be the forge of Vulcan, the Roman god of fire.

Some volcanoes erupt quietly, while others are louder than the greatest explosion ever set off by humans. Volcanoes have the power to destroy, but they are also beautiful, like a fireworks display. Most of us are afraid of their power. But volcanoes are less frightening when you know more about how and when they erupt.

THE PACIFIC RING OF FIRE

Ring of Fire volcanoes occur over one hundred miles behind the deep valleys formed where plates crash together.

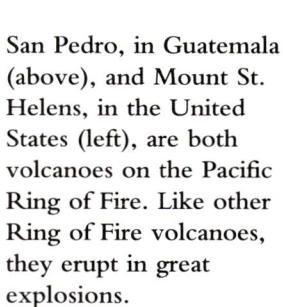

San Pedro, in Guatemala (above), and Mount St. Helens, in the United States (left), are both volcanoes on the Pacific Ring of Fire. Like other Ring of Fire volcanoes, they erupt in great explosions.

The Pacific Ocean is surrounded by explosive volcanoes. These volcanoes form what is called the Pacific Ring of Fire. What is the reason for this feature?

As plate tectonics tells us, North and South America are drifting away from Europe and toward Japan. In fact, all the plates around the Pacific Ocean are moving slowly toward the subduction zones that circle the ocean.

The Ring of Fire volcanoes lie close to these subduction zones. Mount St. Helens and other volcanoes in the northwestern United States lie on the subduction zone between the North American plate and the small Juan de Fuca plate.

The lines of these volcanoes form long, graceful curves, either along the edges of the continents or as chains of islands. Japan is a good example of a volcanic island chain. Japan is made up of about 50 volcanoes along four curved chains. The nearby subduction zone also causes earthquakes.

Millions of people live near the Ring of Fire. They are at risk from sudden eruptions. For their safety, it makes sense to study the way Ring of Fire volcanoes work and to understand them better.

FAMOUS VOLCANIC ERUPTIONS

There have been many volcanic eruptions since people first appeared on earth. The volcano Vesuvius (vuh-SOO-vee-uhs) erupted in the year 79. Vesuvius is in southern Italy, near the city of Naples. Two Roman towns, Pompeii (pahm-PAY) and Herculaneum (HUR-kyuh-LAY-nee-uhm), were built at the foot of Vesuvius.

Thousands of people were killed in this eruption. People running from Pompeii and Herculaneum were buried by falling ash. So were the surrounding farm fields.

Much more recently, a great eruption took place in the western United States. In 1980, Mount St. Helens, in the Cascades mountain chain, erupted. The eruption blew out the side of the volcano and sent rivers of mud and ash flowing out over the countryside. Vast areas of forest were destroyed.

A volcanic eruption can go on for years. The Hawaiian volcano Kilauea began an eruption in 1983 that is still going on. In 1983, *lava* began pouring from a crack in the volcano's side. Lava is magma that comes to the surface in the form of molten rock. It formed a four-mile river that cut through the tropical forest. It burned everything in its path. The lava is still erupting, sometimes in small amounts, sometimes in great rivers.

The eruption of Vesuvius was one of the biggest in history. In two days, Pompeii and Herculaneum were destroyed.

The eruption of Mount St. Helens had more force than any explosion created by humans. Huge amounts of ash were thrown into the sky and thousands of acres of forest were destroyed.

Unlike Mount St. Helens, Kilauea does not erupt with great explosions. Instead, the lava pours out onto the land in great rivers.

STRUCTURE OF A VOLCANO

Some calderas fill with water between eruptions, forming beautiful mountain lakes. Crater Lake, in Oregon, is in a huge caldera.

Volcanoes are a special kind of mountain. Unlike other mountains, such as the Rockies, volcanoes can grow very quickly. In fact, they can grow as much as a thousand feet in just a few months!

Some volcanoes are perfect cones—such as Mount Fujiyama in Japan and Mayon in the Philippines. Others are like great bulging mounds or *shields*—such as the Hawaiian volcanoes and some of those on Iceland or the Galapagos Islands.

How do volcanoes grow? What goes on inside while they are forming? Studying volcanoes from the outside helps scientists find answers to these questions.

Craters are large openings at the tops of volcanoes. Gas, steam, ash, and lava escape through craters. A *caldera* (kawl-DAYR-uh) is a crater that forms when the top of a volcano caves in. Calderas can be many miles across.

Why do craters have many different sizes? A crater's size mainly depends on two things. The first is the type of *vent,* or opening, in earth's crust that allows the eruption to happen and the crater to form. The other is the type of magma that comes up through the crater.

Some volcanoes form wide floods of lava called *fields*—such as the Columbia River plateau of Oregon and Washington.

Usually, the vent is a long crack in the rocks, like a fault. It is hundreds or thousands of feet deep and a few feet across. This crack allows magma to rise and pour out to the surface as lava.

18

Sometimes, magma may come straight to the surface from the mantle. Other times, it gets trapped on the way up. Scientists know that deep inside many volcanoes magma is stored in large spaces called *magma chambers*.

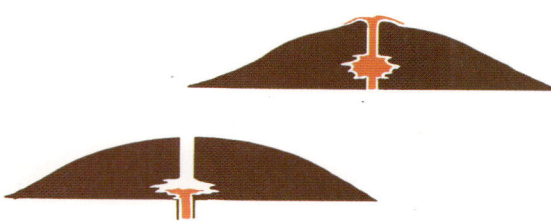

Magma may pass quickly through a magma chamber on its way up, or it may sit and stew for a long time.

Magma does not stay in Kilauea's chamber for long. So, the material that erupts is basically the same as the material that flowed up from the mantle.

The Hawaiian volcano Kilauea has a magma chamber. This chamber is two to four miles below the volcano's summit, or peak. When Kilauea's chamber fills with molten magma rising from below, the volcano bulges outward. It bulges more and more until an eruption releases the pressure. The chamber empties. The volcano settles back down. Another batch of magma begins to collect in the chamber.

Some volcanoes have bigger magma chambers than Kilauea's. Magma may be trapped in a big chamber for a long time. If this happens, the magma may change. For example, magma may take up water as it cools. Also, crystals form and sink to the bottom of the chamber. This makes a volcano explosive.

Devil's Tower, in Wyoming, was once hot magma in an ancient volcano's vent and magma chamber. When the volcano stopped erupting, the magma cooled. Over time, the outer parts of the volcano wore away, and the cooled magma is all that remains.

19

TYPES OF VOLCANIC ERUPTIONS

Fissure eruptions can occur on land. When they do, huge amounts of lava flow onto the earth's surface. This creates *lava fields* that stretch hundreds of miles.

Fissure eruptions have formed huge lava fields in many parts of the world. These fields may be thousands of feet deep.

Central eruptions form tall cone-shaped volcanoes like this one.

Eruptions can be divided into two basic groups: *fissure eruptions* (FISH-ur i-RUHP-shuhnz) and *central eruptions*. Fissure eruptions occur where the crust has pulled apart. The long cracks that form allow magma to rise to the surface. Fissure eruptions are common at ocean ridges and some hot spots, such as Hawaii and Iceland.

Floods of magma have poured through fissure eruptions in parts of the United States, India, Africa, and South America. The magma floods mark places where mantle hot spots split apart old continental plates.

In the Columbia Plateau in Oregon and Washington, lava poured out of fissures 20 million years ago. Nearby hills were buried by a layer of lava over four thousand feet high! The fissures that released the lava can still be seen.

Central eruptions are the best-known kind. Central volcanoes appear all over the world. They are found at ocean ridges, hot spots, and subduction zones. Central volcanoes also occur on land where continents are cracking along faults.

Central eruptions occur in different ways.

Hawaiian eruptions are the most quiet. They are named after the kinds of eruptions seen at the Hawaiian volcanoes. Hawaiian eruptions are most common on hot-spot oceanic islands. The magmas do not contain much water, so they aren't explosive. These eruptions produce lavas that are hot and flow easily. These lavas are called *basaltic* (buh-SAWL-tik) lavas. They form large, smoothly sloping shield volcanoes.

Vulcanian (vuhl-KAY-nee-uhn) eruptions are another type of eruption. They are named after Vulcano, a famous Italian volcano. They can be quite violent. Huge chunks of red-hot lava and cold rock fly into the air. A cloud of gas and ash may rise several miles above the crater.

But *Peleean* (puh-LAY-uhn) eruptions are the most threatening of all. These are named after the 1902 eruption of Mount Pelée (puh-LAY) on the Caribbean island of Martinique.

During that eruption, several glowing gas clouds formed from a series of Vulcanian eruptions in Mount Pelée. Then, a plug of thick, sticky magma grew inside the volcano. It exploded with such force that a glowing white-hot gas cloud blew sideways through Mount Pelée.

The eruptions of Mount St. Helens in 1980 (above) and Mount Lassen in 1915 (right) were both *Vesuvian* (vuh-SOO-vee-uhn). A Vesuvian eruption is even more powerful than a Vulcanian eruption.

The lava and other materials that are put out by a central eruption build the volcano higher and higher around the vent.

Mount Etna, on the island of Sicily, is more explosive than a Hawaiian volcano, but less explosive than a Vesuvian volcano.

WHAT COMES OUT OF VOLCANOES

In this picture, you can see two types of basaltic lava. *Aa* (AH-ah), at the top of the picture, forms a rough, blocky crust as it cools. *Pahoehoe* (puh-HO-ay-HO-ay), at the bottom of the picture, forms a smooth crust like the skin on a pudding.

There are two main types of volcanic rocks. The first is lava, which is erupted magma. The second type, called *pyroclastic* (PY-ro-KLAS-tik) rocks, are broken bits of solid rock.

Basaltic lavas are runny and black. These lavas form shield volcanoes and flood eruptions because they can flow very far. When a basalt flow begins to cool, it forms a crust. The crust may be fairly smooth, like the skin that forms on pudding. Or, it may have a thick, rough surface containing loose blocks of solid lava.

When basaltic lava erupts on the sea floor, it forms small lumps. The lumps cool quickly, forming a glassy surface. These lumps are called "pillows" because they're about the same size and shape as pillows we sleep on.

Rhyolite (RY-uh-LYT) is the stickiest, thickest type of lava. It's usually white. This thick lava forms a rounded roof or a sticky plug over the vent. Rhyolite can sometimes explode if gas and water are trapped inside.

Andesite (AN-di-ZYT) is another type of lava. Its amount of stickiness falls between basaltic and rhyolite lavas. It is often greenish-grey in color. Andesite is the most common lava released from Ring of Fire volcanoes.

Some volcanoes erupt only one kind of rock. Others may spit out many different types of rock in a short time.

These rocks are cooled andesite lava. Andesite is named after the Andes Mountains in South America.

22

Pyroclastic Rocks and Pyroclastic Flows

Ash is the finest type of pyroclastic rock. It is released during most kinds of eruptions. Eruptions that are more explosive release more ash. Ash is made up of tiny particles thrown high into the air by a volcano. Falling ash can be like dust.

Blocks and *bombs* are larger pieces of pyroclastic rock. They are usually made of chunks of cooled lava. Blocks are already solid rock when they are erupted. Bombs are blobs of molten lava that cool as they fall to earth. Both can be thrown miles away from a volcano by the force of an eruption.

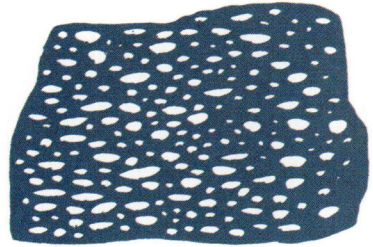

Pumice (PUHM-uhs) is a glassy rock that's very light because it has many holes. The holes are formed by popping gas bubbles. Pumice is so light, it can be blown high into the sky.

Pyroclastic rocks do not just get blown into the sky. Mud or ash may form *pyroclastic flows* during a violent eruption. Some volcanoes are famous for flows like these. Pyroclastic flows can move with great speed and cause much damage.

Volcanic blocks can weigh up to hundreds of pounds. Imagine the force needed to throw such a large object into the air!

After an eruption, chunks of pumice have been found floating in the ocean!

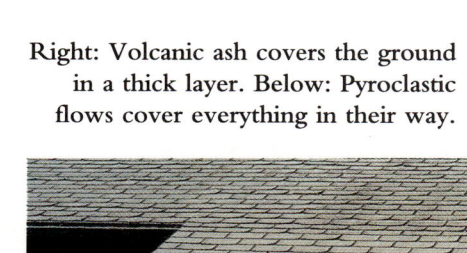
Right: Volcanic ash covers the ground in a thick layer. Below: Pyroclastic flows cover everything in their way.

SIDE EFFECTS OF ERUPTIONS

In Nicaragua, gases from the Masaya (muh-SY-uh) volcano ruined coffee plantations even before an eruption started.

Cars and factories pollute the air we breathe. So, we try to cut down on pollution coming from these sources. But pollution from volcanoes is an even bigger problem! Still, there is little we can do except to study and understand this form of pollution.

Some eruptions coat the area around them with a layer of dirty ash. People's houses, cars, and yards are covered with it.

Gas is probably the worst danger that comes from volcanoes—even when they are not erupting. One reason these gases are so dangerous is that they are heavier than air. So, the gases sink and cling to the ground when blown from a volcano. They mix with the air that living things breathe.

Our environment is a fragile balance between events deep in the earth and events at the surface. Volcanoes affect this balance in many ways.

Sudden eruptions can bury whole towns before people can escape. This is what happened to the towns of Pompeii and Herculaneum in Italy nearly two thousand years ago.

The blasts from an erupting volcano beneath the sea can also cause huge waves in oceans and seas nearby. These waves are called *tsunamis* (soo-NAHM-eez). When they reach land, tsunamis can cause damage thousands of miles away, across the ocean from a volcano!

Pompeii and Herculaneum were not found again until almost two thousand years after they were buried.

Erupting volcanoes can also change the weather. A great eruption pushes huge amounts of ash into the atmosphere. Ash can darken the sky for weeks. Winds can spread it very far.

In 1883, the volcano Krakatoa erupted enormous amounts of ash. Krakatoa is in Indonesia. In just a few days, the dusty ash had spread to South Africa and the southern Atlantic Ocean. The ash kept moving west. The winds carried it across South America and the Pacific Ocean. Finally, the ash cloud had completely circled the globe. In fact, it did this several times!

As the cloud blew west it also began spreading north. In time, it colored the skies over Europe, Asia, and North America. Brilliant red and golden sunsets appeared wherever the ash cloud spread.

We should remember that volcanoes' effects on the environment are not all harmful. Volcanic ash slowly turns into soil that is very good for farming. This is one reason that many people make their homes on the slopes of volcanoes, even though they know about the dangers of eruptions.

Above: The land around volcanoes is very rich and good for farming. This is why many people live near volcanoes. Left: Ash from an eruption can fall out of the air and become trapped in layers of snow and ice far from the volcano.

The effects of one eruption can be felt around the world.

The side effects of volcanic ash are not always ugly. Ash in the atmosphere can cause brilliantly colored sunsets.

EARTHQUAKES can be very strong. Or, they can be so weak people hardly notice them. Did you ever feel the ground move, or tremble, when a train or heavy truck passed by? Imagine a trembling hundreds or thousands of times more powerful, and you have some idea about what a strong earthquake feels like.

Earthquakes result from movements along faults in the earth's crust. Like volcanoes, they tell us of the huge forces within our living planet.

Scientists locate and study more than 150,000 earthquakes each year. They use special machines to measure the sizes of earthquakes. "Listening in" to earthquakes with these machines tells scientists what's happening deep within the earth.

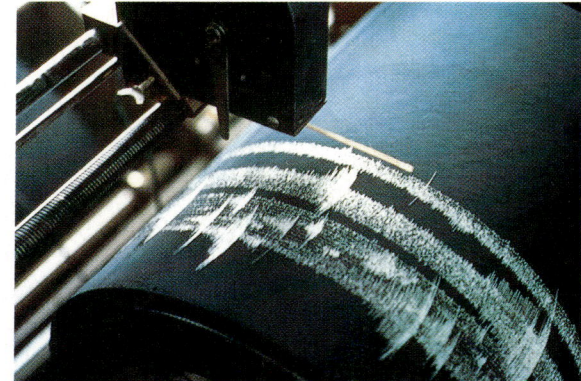

FAULTS

A normal fault has caused the rocks on the left side of the picture to drop down. If you look carefully, you can see the line of the fault in the rock layers.

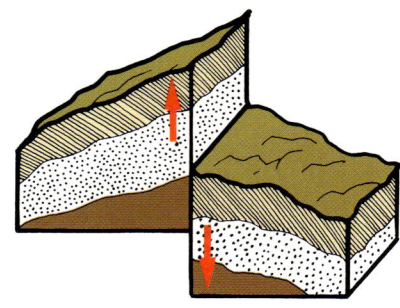

Some of the longest faults form where two plates come together. Faults can also be found within tectonic plates.

Right: This cliff is a scarp at the edge of the East African Rift Valley, an ancient rift valley on the African continent. Below: In this photo, you can see how the earth's surface drops down on one side of a normal fault when the crust is stretched.

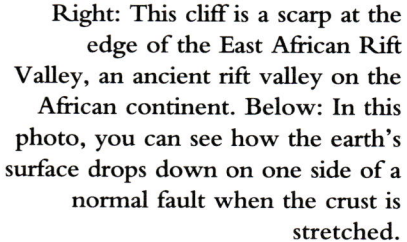

Imagine dropping a pebble into the water. The pebble causes a splash, then ripples fan out in all directions. The ripples are a sign that the pebble's splash created energy. The energy spreads through the water in waves.

Movements in the earth's crust along faults also release energy. The energy spreads through the earth in the form of an earthquake, just as the energy from dropping the pebble spreads through the water as ripples.

Scientists map faults through careful study of surface features and sudden changes in the rock. There are three types of faults: *normal faults, thrust faults,* and *strike-slip faults.* Let's look at each type.

Normal faults show up-and-down movements along the fault. The fault forms when the crust stretches until it breaks. Crust moves up on one side and down on the other side of the fault. As a result, one side of the fault is higher than the other. The steep edge of the higher side is called a *scarp*.

Sometimes two normal faults form a *rift valley.* Rift valleys are closed in by normal faults facing opposite directions. We see these at ocean ridges and within the continents.

Thrust faults show up-and-down movement as normal faults do. But thrust faults form in a different way. They appear when the crust cracks from being squashed together under pressure, not from being stretched.

If rocks cannot fold under pressure, they will crack. Rocks on one side of the crack will be thrust, or pushed, over those on the other side. This may sound familiar—remember how tectonic plates bump into each other at subduction zones? One plate is thrust over another. Subduction zones are simply large thrust faults!

Strike-slip faults are different from normal and thrust faults. There is no up-and-down movement of the sides of strike-slip faults. Instead, the fault's sides move sideways past one another. Strike-slip faults form transform plate boundaries. The San Andreas Fault is a good example. Strike-slip faults also occur cutting across ocean ridges.

Some earthquakes happen in the middle of tectonic plates instead of at their edges. These earthquakes may mark hot spots deep in the mantle. Or, they could be caused by an ancient plate trying to crack apart.

Left: The city of Los Angeles is close to the San Andreas Fault, a strike-slip fault. Below: When rocks are pushed together, they break, just like this road. This is how thrust faults are formed.

A fault may be *active* or *inactive*. A fault is called active if it produces earthquakes. Inactive faults do not show any movement.

This strike-slip fault cuts right across a field. You can see how the sides of the fault have moved over time.

STRUCTURE OF AN EARTHQUAKE

This crack is all you can see at the surface of a fault in the crust. When this fault shifts, it will send vibrations through the crust that make up an earthquake.

Earthquakes are vibrations, or waves, in the rocks. As they travel through the crust, these waves can rattle windows or shatter buildings, depending on their power. When earthquake waves move through soft soils, they grow in size. This is why earthquakes do so much damage when passing through parts of cities like San Francisco, Tokyo, or Mexico City. These cities have mud or other soft layers beneath them.

Understanding earthquake waves helps scientists see how earthquakes work. There are three types of earthquake waves.

Primary waves vibrate in the direction in which the waves travel. Imagine a spring like the kind you find inside a sofa. Imagine it stretching out and springing back. This is similar to the way primary waves move.

Earthquake waves are usually too small to be seen. But they vibrate so quickly that they shake and break things in their path.

Both Tokyo (above) and San Francisco (right) are built on soft soils. For this reason, earthquakes can do great damage to these cities.

Secondary waves move through all parts of the earth. They vibrate at right angles to the direction the waves travel. Secondary waves move up and down like the folds of a flag flapping in the wind. This movement can do much damage to buildings.

Surface waves are like ocean waves. They move along the earth's surface. They affect only rocks in the upper part of the crust. Surface waves also cause damage.

30

If you bend a stick, it snaps. Something similar happens before and during an earthquake. While the stick is bending, it stores energy. When it snaps, the energy is suddenly released. The broken ends of the stick quiver and send out sound waves. Earthquakes work much the same way.

People have actually seen roads, fences, and railroad lines built across faults slowly bend as pressure builds

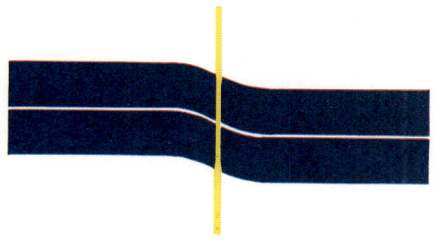

along the fault. When the rock below cracks suddenly (like a breaking stick), the fault moves—and an earthquake begins!

The *focus* is the point in the crust where the slip begins and the earthquake waves start. The point above the focus, up top on the surface, is called the *epicenter* (EP-i-SEN-tur). Scientists find an earthquake's focus and its epicenter by using a machine called a *seismometer* (syz-MAHM-uh-tur). They measure how long it takes primary and secondary waves to be picked up by the machine.

The focus of a deep earthquake may be four or five hundred miles down. Deep earthquakes are not very common. Shallow earthquakes are more common. They are caused by faults within the crust.

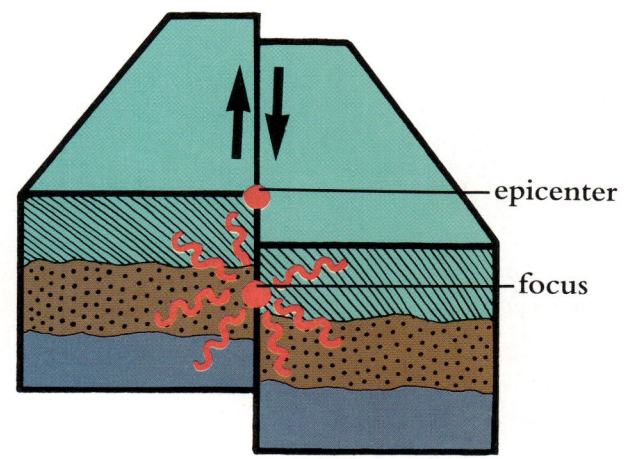

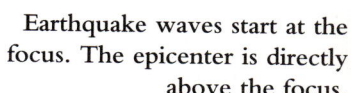

Earthquake waves start at the focus. The epicenter is directly above the focus.

Some earthquakes have their focus point in the mantle. Others have their focus point in the crust. It's important to know where the focus of an earthquake is.

Above: Farther away from an earthquake's epicenter, there is less damage. Right: This town was close to an earthquake's epicenter. It was nearly destroyed by the shaking.

MEASURING EARTHQUAKES

The greater the intensity of an earthquake, the more it affects people's lives and their environment.

People in tall buildings will probably be the first to feel an earthquake's shaking.

Only sensitive instruments pick up earthquake waves that have an intensity of 1.

An earthquake with an intensity of 6 or 7 can shake the bricks off the outside of a building.

How strong is an earthquake? That's a question scientists are always interested in answering. The strength of an earthquake is called its *intensity*.

Scientists use the modified Mercalli scale to describe the intensity of an earthquake. The higher the number, the stronger the earthquake. On the modified Mercalli scale, "1" stands for the weakest earthquake and "12" stands for the strongest.

Let's take a closer look at what type of earthquake each number stands for.

1. This is the weakest measurable earthquake.

2. The earthquake is felt by a few people, mostly in the upper parts of buildings. Anything hanging will start to swing.

3. The earthquake is felt indoors and in parked cars, which may rock slightly.

4. The earthquake is felt by many people indoors, and by some outdoors. People may hear doors and windows rattle.

5. The earthquake is felt by most people. Dishes and windows may break. Objects may fall over.

6. The earthquake is felt by everyone. Heavy furniture may shift around. Plaster ceilings often fall.

7. Many ordinary buildings are damaged or destroyed.

8. The earthquake destroys ordinary buildings. Only well-made buildings escape damage.

9. The earthquake damages even sturdy buildings. Some will collapse.

10. The earthquake smashes most buildings. The ground cracks badly.

11. The earthquake leaves few buildings standing. Railroad tracks are bent and large cracks appear in the ground.

12. This is the strongest earthquake possible. It causes almost complete destruction.

Complete destruction like this is caused by earthquakes with intensities of 10 or more.

The intensity of an earthquake and the amount of damage it causes depend on three things: the amount of energy released, the distance of a town from the epicenter, and the type of rock involved.

Scientists who study earthquakes also try to answer questions about their size, apart from the damage they cause. This earthquake measurement is called *magnitude* (MAG-nuh-TOOD).

The *Richter scale* is used to describe magnitude. A "0" on the Richter scale means that no earthquake waves are being measured. There is no maximum number on the scale.

The greatest magnitude ever measured for an earthquake is 8.8. This magnitude seems to be about the highest possible.

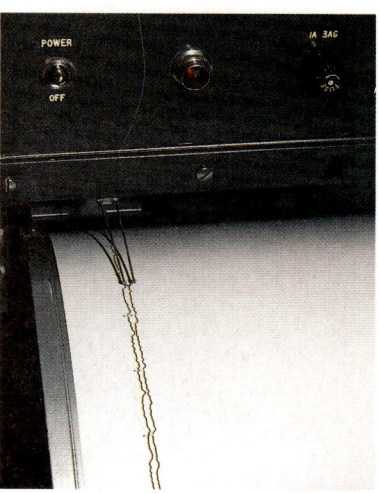

An earthquake's magnitude depends on the size of the earthquake waves as measured by a seismometer.

Even when an earthquake does not cause total destruction, the damage can make it difficult for people to lead their daily lives.

TSUNAMIS

In the open ocean, people would not feel a tsunami passing beneath them. When the same wave hits the shore, it could be 90 feet high!

People living on the Pacific coast and around the Mediterranean Sea must watch constantly for tsunamis caused by distant earthquakes.

This ship was carried far from the place where it was anchored by the power of a tsunami.

Sometimes, a large fault moves under the ocean floor. The movement causes an unusual water wave called a tsunami. Tsunamis cross the ocean at very high speeds. They sometimes rush along at hundreds of miles per hour. The most dangerous tsunamis are caused by large fault movements at subduction zones.

Tsunamis travel fast enough to cross whole oceans in a few hours! Tsunami waves are not very high in the open ocean, though. They only measure a few inches high or so.

As tsunamis approach land, the waves pack closer together. They rise even higher—even up to ninety feet! That's as tall as a nine-story building! When these waves hit the shore they can cause terrible damage.

One set of tsunamis hit Hawaii on April 1, 1946. These tsunami waves could hardly be seen at sea. They did not even affect ships in their path. Yet their speed was about five hundred miles an hour!

The 20-foot-high tsunamis reached the Hawaiian Islands in less than five hours. The waves arrived about twelve minutes apart. They swept over the land, destroying trees, houses, and crops in their path.

FAMOUS EARTHQUAKES

Some of the best-known earthquakes of this century have happened in California. One of the most famous earthquakes occurred in 1906 in San Francisco. At that time, San Francisco was the state's biggest city.

What caused this earthquake? As you might have guessed, it was a sharp movement along the San Andreas Fault. The fault's sides moved as much as 18 feet in some places.

You may remember hearing about another earthquake that shook San Francisco in 1989. By this time, San Francisco was a far bigger city than it was in 1906. The nearby Bay Area was covered with houses, factories, freeways, and bridges.

Rush hour was just beginning at about 5 P.M. on October 10, 1989. The World Series was about to begin in San Francisco's baseball stadium. A few minutes after five o'clock, a sharp earthquake hit the Bay Area.

This was not as big an earthquake as in 1906. Still, it was a disaster for many people in San Francisco and nearby towns. Scientists say that California could be hit by another earthquake as strong as the 1906 earthquake, and that it could happen someday soon! The San Andreas Fault is a very active plate boundary carefully watched by scientists.

On October 10, 1989, one of the largest earthquakes since 1906 occurred in San Francisco.

Right: In 1906, San Francisco was almost completely destroyed by the earthquake. Below: The earthquake of 1989 did less damage, but the collapse of an important freeway caused many problems.

LIVING WITH DANGER

is a habit for many people. We have seen how volcanoes and earthquakes work. What scientists learn from studying these things helps pinpoint which regions are dangerous to live in. It also helps people spot signs of a disaster in the making.

If scientists warn of danger, people can move their families and belongings in good time. Many lives can be saved. But sometimes, disaster arrives without warning. Then, countries around the world send help to the affected area. They may send medicine, food, or machines to help rebuild the damaged buildings.

What happens after a disaster is also part of the story.

STUDYING THE EARTH

Kilauea is a fairly quiet, "well-behaved" volcano. Scientists can walk right up to a lava flow and take pictures!

Scientists who study volcanoes are called *volcanologists* (VAHL-kuh-NAHL-uh-juhsts). Many volcanologists work in countries like Japan and Italy, where volcanoes are a constant threat. In the United States, the Volcano Observatory in Hawaii is a famous center for the study of volcanoes. There, volcanologists use the natural laboratory of Kilauea.

Scientists can study lava samples easily. They look at them under a microscope to find out what mineral crystals they contain. The mineral mixture gives clues about where the magma was formed and what might be erupted later.

Studies of volcanoes and earthquakes go hand in hand. Earthquake measurements are an important part of studying the activity and inner workings of volcanoes.

Sometimes scientists must go right up to flows of red-hot lava. They take samples of the lava by poking a metal pole into the lava and twisting it. Blobs of lava stick to the rod and cool quickly.

Scientists who study earthquakes are called *seismologists* (syz-MAHL-uh-juhsts). Like volcanologists, seismologists keep a close eye on active faults. They use seismometers to measure the magnitudes of earthquakes. They also have special measuring instruments that show slow ground movements along a fault.

Seismologists collect information about faults from all around the globe. The information is fed into computers. The computers map earthquakes that have happened in distant regions. The maps show where tectonic plates are most active.

Seismometers placed around the world send earthquake information to scientists in their laboratories.

PREDICTING ERUPTIONS

Volcanologists have two important goals. The first is to predict, or know ahead of time, the place and time of a future eruption. The second goal is to learn how explosive a volcano is. If scientists know a volcano's history, they have a much better chance of meeting their goals when studying that volcano. Still, the job of a volcanologist is not easy!

Mount Hood is considered dormant because it has not erupted for centuries. Still, it could suddenly begin to erupt, as Mount St. Helens did.

Volcanic eruptions seem to follow three main patterns. The first is random. This means the volcano seems to erupt without any pattern at all. This kind of eruption is the hardest to predict.

The second pattern is more regular. As time goes on, the volcano is more likely to erupt. In other words, once it starts erupting there is a strong chance it will continue with further eruptions.

Volcanoes that follow the third pattern erupt at regular periods. The period of time between eruptions may get longer as years go by. Once a team of volcanologists has decided which eruption pattern a volcano fits, they can try to figure out when the next eruption might start.

Right: Scientists do not yet know the pattern of Mount St. Helens' eruptions. The 1980 eruption was the first in centuries. Below: Mount Ngauruhoe, in New Zealand, erupts in a fairly regular pattern.

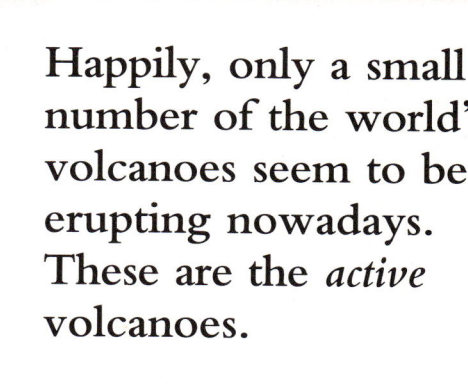

Happily, only a small number of the world's volcanoes seem to be erupting nowadays. These are the *active* volcanoes.

PREDICTING EARTHQUAKES

Predicting earthquakes can't prevent damage to property. But, if people can be warned in time, a correct prediction could save thousands of lives.

Seismologists have tried different ways in the last 30 years to make useful predictions.

The San Andreas Fault is one of the most carefully watched faults in the world. Because so many people live nearby, it is important to try to predict when it will cause an earthquake.

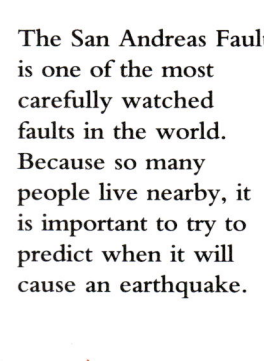

Predicting earthquakes is harder than predicting volcanic eruptions. Earthquakes have been predicted by using many different methods. But no one method seems to work every time.

The most promising idea for predicting earthquakes has been *elastic rebound*. After an earthquake, the pressure starts building up again along a fault. Scientists try to measure this pressure and how fast it is building. They calculate how much pressure it takes to cause a major earthquake. They use this information to predict when the next major earthquake should happen.

Another sign of earthquake activity is the leaking of radon gas. Radon is a radioactive gas contained in the rocks in the crust of the earth. Scientists are working on ways to use radon as a signal for predicting upcoming earthquakes.

One large earthquake, in northern China on February 4, 1975, was correctly predicted. Years before, the Chinese government had started a special program. People who lived near big faults were asked to watch for warning signs of earthquakes. For example, people watched for changes in the water level in wells. They also kept an eye on their farm animals. Many people think animals feel unusual earth movements before humans.

PROTECTING AGAINST DISASTER

People in places like Japan and the western United States have learned much about building houses that can survive earthquakes. Wood-frame houses of one or two stories have a good chance of getting through an earthquake with little damage. These houses should also be built on a solid base of strong concrete. Of course, there are also many tall buildings in the big cities of Japan and California. These buildings are made of special materials that can withstand earthquakes. They are also built using methods that help buildings survive the ground shaking.

There are other ways people protect themselves against earthquakes. They make sure their stoves, refrigerators, and other electrical equipment are attached to the floor. If a stove falls over, it can cause a fire. People also tie heavy furniture down so that it won't crash around during an earthquake.

One of the best types of protection is to avoid building your home too close to a volcano or a fault. But sometimes people go ahead and build in unsafe areas because they think the danger is over. Often, it is hard to tell whether a volcano or fault is really inactive.

In the shadow of Mount Fujiyama, these traditional farmhouses show the building methods the Japanese used to make houses that could survive Japan's frequent earthquakes and eruptions.

With the help of scientists, people have learned how to build buildings that can survive earthquakes.

Above: The porch is one part of the house that is often damaged in an earthquake. Right: Modern materials and building methods make it possible for people to build tall apartment buildings, like this one, in places like Japan and California.

AFTER A DISASTER

Even a lava flow from a "quiet" Hawaiian eruption can cause much damage and disrupt people's lives.

Can volcanic eruptions cause some kinds of animals to become extinct, or disappear? Some scientists believe this has happened at least once in history.

An erupting volcano may change the weather by blotting out the sun with a cloud of ash. The effects of an eruption are not just local. They can be seen thousands of miles away.

As far back as 1783, people were exploring the ways volcanoes affect weather. An American inventor named Benjamin Franklin was one of those people. In 1783, the volcano Laki erupted in Iceland. Mr. Franklin noticed that fog covered much of the earth for months. Also, the winter was colder than usual.

Many scientists believe large eruptions cause cooler weather. They think ash in the atmosphere keeps the warming sunlight from getting through. Some scientists even think volcanoes made the world's weather cold enough to cause long periods of ice and snow, the earth's Ice Ages.

Not everyone agrees, though. Dust clouds from a volcano might also trap heat near the surface of the earth. This heat would normally escape back into the atmosphere. As a result, volcanoes might make the weather warmer!

Some scientists believe eruptions can strongly affect animal life. They think pollution from a huge eruption could have changed the land and weather so much that the dinosaurs could no longer survive.

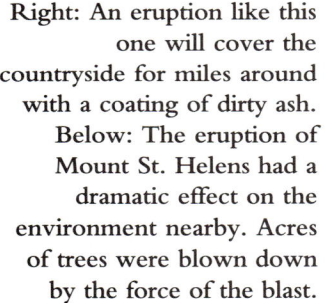

Right: An eruption like this one will cover the countryside for miles around with a coating of dirty ash. Below: The eruption of Mount St. Helens had a dramatic effect on the environment nearby. Acres of trees were blown down by the force of the blast.

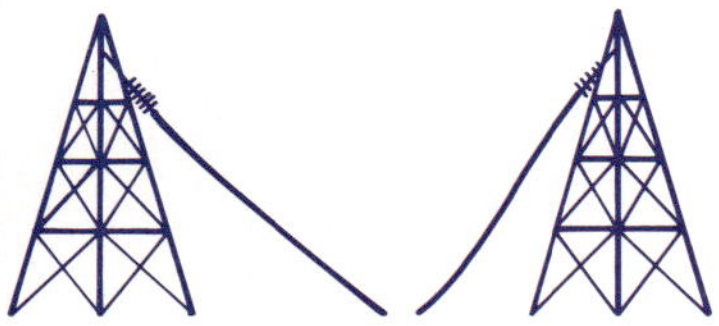

Earthquakes bring people's lives to a standstill, just as volcanoes do. They destroy buildings and all kinds of property. They break power lines, throwing whole cities into darkness. And, most important, they can hurt and kill people.

No matter where an earthquake happens, people try to set up a rescue effort. A good rescue effort takes planning and care. It takes trucks and helicopters and roads to get to the location. Sometimes, all of these things are in place. If they are not, it is harder to reach people who need help and to treat them.

Rescuers must move very quickly and carefully to save lives. People who are rescued must be moved away. Rescuers must then make sure people do not return before the danger has gone.

Volcanic eruptions and earthquakes can pollute a town's drinking water. It's important to make sure people drink only clean water. Doctors can help by giving shots to fight many diseases. People who are hurt must be taken to a hospital for treatment.

Our amazing planet has many surprises in store for us. But, by learning more about it, we can help make all parts of the earth safer for the people who live there.

One of the first things rescuers do is try to reach people trapped in fallen buildings, landslides, or mudflows.

An earthquake or volcanic eruption can affect the lives of people nearby for years to come. That is why it is important to know as much as we can about these natural wonders.

Here, an oil pipeline has broken and oil is leaking into the ground after an earthquake. This is dangerous because the oil could pollute the drinking water. It could also start fires.

A disaster may make thousands of people homeless. After the 1906 earthquake in San Francisco, people set up a city of tents to live in.

GLOSSARY

Caldera (kahl-DAYR-uh): A very large crater that forms when the upper part of a volcano collapses.

Core: The innermost part of the earth, surrounded by the mantle and crust. The outer part of the core is liquid. Its inner part is solid.

Crater: The hole at the top of a volcano where the main vent brings magma to the surface.

Crust: The outermost layer of the earth. The crust lies beneath the continents and the ocean floors.

Dormant (DOR-muhnt): This really means "sleeping." It describes a volcano that has not erupted in a long time, but may still begin to erupt at any moment.

Earthquake: A sudden movement of the earth's crust, usually along a crack, or fault.

Epicenter (EP-i-SENT-ur): The point at the surface of the earth's crust directly above the focus, the spot within the crust or mantle where an earthquake begins.

Fault: A crack in the earth's crust. Movement along a fault causes earthquakes.

Focus: The point within the crust or mantle where a fault movement starts an earthquake. It lies below the epicenter.

Hot spot: A part of the earth's surface above an extra-hot part of the mantle. At hot spots, blobs of hot magma force their way from the mantle up through the crust and form volcanoes at the surface.

Intensity: The force of an earthquake measured by the amount of damage done.

Lava: Molten rock erupted by volcanoes.

Magma (MAG-muh): Molten rock from the mantle or crust. When magma reaches the surface through eruptions, it becomes lava.

Magnitude (MAG-nuh-TOOD): A measure of the amount of energy given out by an earthquake. Magnitude is measured on the Richter scale.

Mantle: The part of the earth that separates the core from the crust. The mantle is solid rock, but because it is under extreme pressure, it can flow like putty.

Ocean ridge: A range of undersea mountains that stretches across the sea floor. Ocean ridges are formed where new plates are formed by magma coming up from the mantle.

Plate boundary: Places where tectonic plates meet. Plates may crash into each other, move away from each other, or move alongside each other at plate boundaries.

Plate tectonics (tek-TAHN-ihks): The process of plates moving across the earth. Plate tectonics is probably driven by movements of the mantle below.

Primary wave: An earthquake wave that moves in the direction in which it travels, like a spring coiling and stretching.

Secondary wave: An earthquake wave that moves at right angles to the direction in which it travels, like a flag flapping in the wind.

Subduction (suhb-DUHK-shuhn): When two tectonic plates crash into each other, one dives beneath the other, back into the mantle. This process is called subduction. It causes earthquakes and volcanoes.

Surface waves: Earthquake waves that move across the land's surface.

Tectonic (tek-TANH-ik) **plate**: A piece of the earth's crust that moves across the earth's surface, bumping into or scraping against other plates.

Transform plate boundary: The boundary between two plates that are neither crashing into each other nor moving apart.

Tsunami (soo-NAHM-ee): A large ocean wave caused by a fault movement or a volcanic eruption on the ocean floor.

Volcano: A place on the earth's surface where lava, ash, and steam erupt onto the surface and into the atmosphere. Volcanoes can be quiet or very explosive.